The Butcher's Granddaughter

by

Adela Sinclair

Finishing Line Press
Georgetown, Kentucky

The Butcher's Granddaughter

Copyright © 2025 by Adela Sinclair
ISBN 979-8-89990-029-7 First Edition
All rights reserved under International and Pan-American Copyright Conventions. No part of this book may be reproduced in any manner whatsoever without written permission from the publisher, except in the case of brief quotations embodied in critical articles and reviews.

Publisher: Leah Huete de Maines
Editor: Christen Kincaid
Cover Art and Design: Alisha Hawrylyszyn Frank
Author Photo: Shoshana Spencer
Cover Design: Elizabeth Maines McCleavy

Order online: www.finishinglinepress.com
 also available on amazon.com

>Author inquiries and mail orders:
>Finishing Line Press
>PO Box 1626
>Georgetown, Kentucky 40324
>USA

Contents

Între trecut și tăcere—Between the Past and Silence 1
His Hands 3
The Butcher 6
Dedi and the Neighbor 7
Hungry? 8
Topogan 9
Dedi's Absence 10
Buni's Silence 11
In the Beginning 13
Our House 15
Circle of the Sun 17
This is How I Ran Away At Seven 19
I Grew And Grew at Nine… 20
I Left My House 23
Spoon 24
Mama's Green Bike 26
Dad's Ways 27
Hansel & Gretel 28
Reins Of Time And Dust 30
I Send Courage To The Moon 37
I Don't Know How To Write A Story 38
April 12, 2018 41
In The Gut 42
April 11, 2018 43
The Prince And The Game 44
Yearning For Light 46
If They Smile Kiss Them For Me 48
I Cannot Lie 50

No Witness Will Ever Read This 53
Unmasked Truth.. 54
By Time, Sorrow, And Life 56
I Am My Father's Daughter... 57
My Fear, My Butcher, My Love... 59
I Pray For Sinners 60

Între trecut și tăcere—Between the Past and Silence

Îmi amintesc—I remember

I remember Adi's dad bursting through the classroom doors, throwing his son between rows of desks and kicking him hard. We were in 2nd grade.

I remember the milkman coming to our house. He would drop off the bottles by our front door. I remember pasteurizing the milk in our kitchen. The milk bottle caps we'd turn into silver stars to decorate our Christmas Tree.

I remember in high school wanting to wear only brown for the rest of my life. I remember shopping at the local thrift store and eating a BLT each Friday, from the corner Deli.

I remember my first color TV. It was during the 1984 Olympics. We were glued to the screen for a couple of days.

I remember eating the same thing for lunch each day for at least 10 years. Lard on dry bread with salt and paprika.

I remember getting my period for the first time. I was wearing pink tights. The blood stained them. When I was in the bathroom and took them off, I yelled with surprise.

I remember sitting at the coffee shop with dad and Alex and by the time the waitress brought the ice cream, it had melted. Nowadays, I place my bowl in the microwave to recreate it.

I remember when the ambulance hit the motorcyclist. He fell out of his seat directly on his head. I remember dad ran to help. The man's head was bleeding, in the middle of the street. He lay there, in a pool of his own blood. We had dropped our bags of peanuts on the sidewalk.

I remember rose petal juice, sometimes pink, other times yellow, depending on the roses that flowered in our yard.

I remember the changing room at the outdoor pool. It was made of wooden planks, plenty of space for eyes to see you changing.

I remember becoming self conscious of my naked body.

I remember melting into the pool, sinking underwater. How my nostrils filled with water.

I remember the green gate of our house and knowing who came home by how they slammed the gate.

I remember pig's ears fresh off a pig's head. Sinking my teeth into them. Charred and chewy.

I remember the first really bad bicycle accident I had.

I remember acculturation vs. assimilation.

I remember the taste of lard and salt, the charred pig's ears, and the way my body changed under those wooden planks.

Acculturation taught me to remember.

Assimilation begged me to forget.

I remember.

His Hands

His hands were reddened and blueish. Through his veins there were particles of truth. The neat fibrous squares being cut away from the sow's skeleton. His hands were complex hands, hands that knew. How to cut. How to hurt till death. His hands were anatomical. His body betrayed me with its strength when all I craved was tenderness. Words did not meet me halfway. Hands did not hold me, but rubbed my belly after eating. My hand offered an apple slice, would he take it? Held out with glossy fingers. He thought of snakes. The scent made him forget the terror. His terror. The anatomical terror of the sow, under the sharp knife in his hands. The green gate he slammed daily, hands on the handles of the bike he rode home from the butcher shop. Tissue and fluid inside the black leather case with a red lining. Meat was also there. Our food for days. Fingers that betrayed. Looking at him, he was perhaps 50, a man who carried his age rather than bore it. What he carried he did not try to hide. The garden was a tank whose glass case held the sun hostage and rays of orange-gold bled for hours. We sat on the bench where the grass was soaked.

Had he killed today? Cut today? Measured with uninflected pace the pacing of the dying animal? The dying animal was in his hands. Every day a new animal is at his fingertips. At his mercy. At the mercy of hungry mothers that wanted to feed their crying children. Purple is how I see his hands. Through the coma and dying of the light, I looked at him. In the train station that night. I left my entire town behind. On the train platform saying goodbye one last time. On the *peron*. How I administer the meaning of love to him. First love, hankering for safety, longing for something with an escape route built in. I loved my scarecrow-for-birds of a grandfather. I began to fall asleep on the gray seat next to him. Safety of falling. By the time I reached his age and even older, that memory allowed me to recreate his image while an ocean apart.

His hands were gifts, as gold coins rattled musically falling to the ground. Wealth of knowing he was always going to come home to me. He had a thick throat. The sow had a thick throat. I sat there next to him on the bench in the backyard. The orchard was right here surrounding us. I reached my hand and grabbed a red apple.

When he asked, I would choke with him. I would choke on the apple that I offered. He would bite savagely, choke next, in the tendons of lost-addressed and burned paintings. He denounced his Communist affiliation, but was burdened with the loss that came with them, the Securitate. His friends constantly disappeared. They would not return to their families and homes. The families spoke Hungarian, I did not understand. Hungarian was the adults' secret language. They were able to convey the pain of the disappearances of all those men and women. Suddenly, the neighbor did not lean on her window sill in the front of his house ever again. The adults wondered where her body might be.

Early evening on December 25th, 1989, Ceaușescu was boo-ed while he gave his inordinate speech for the millionth time. A day later he was executed after escaping. The bullet went into the front of his head. Executed on live TV. French television.

I was 15, in Paris, when this happened. His fingers twitched as he hit the ground. His wife Elena followed. This is how Communism fell on Christmas in Romania. The bodies of our neighbors, our parent's friends were found buried in the ground alongside many other bodies. I remember their feet vividly. The bodies—anatomical experiments. Now, the truth unearthed and light shed upon their longtime disappearances. The feet had five snakehead toes. The nails of each toe pulled out of the nail bed with plyers. That's how they died. Gushing blood through extremities. Fingers and toes, the size of large brown potatoes. Inflamed by their hour of death.

And he, Ceaușescu, in one bullet, was gone. Maybe his eyes needed to be gouged out with pliers or a butter knife. Then plopped on top of a lamppost to look over the casualties found, all laid out of their graves on the ground. His thick throat choked on the carnage. This mass autopsy, a live performance. In front of all of us.

Did the world pay attention? I was 15, enthralled by the events. I had not been able to fend off nightmares. Paris was so beautiful. Covered in snow. Under the lights of the Champs Elysee. It would have killed me to be in Romania at the time, on the steps of the Church in Timisoara square. That is where many died, choking bullets hit them. I was surrounded by architectural beauty. All I saw were bridges breaking and his palace crumbling. Shots were fired. The Securitate tank killed a French reporter. Ran him over. They ran us all over. Then, silence. Women's weeping stopped. The profundity of spoken words became meaningless.

I look down at my small feet, at Dedi's fingers, reddish and curled in a fist. He is sleeping in the garden, the sun a deeper shade of red.

The Butcher

Dedi cuts meticulously. He holds an oversized knife in his right hand, the veins protrude and pulsate with blue through the reddened skin. His large hands, encompassing the dark handle fully. When he cuts he stands out of his chair at the kitchen table. I always sit across from him and can study his severe face each day, each meal. Work does not interfere with us eating together which is a curse. It is in America we strive for as a family to accomplish and cannot. This is the hand that rubs my belly.

After he feeds me he asks me: "Come to Dedi, Adeluța. Sit in my lap... let me check, did you eat enough?" Sad blue eyes light up. My belly is concave. His hand is a shovel that taps on the ground of a freshly buried body. Dedi's cuts are deadly. In minutes, the struggling animal is silent. Neck cut, head flaps backwards, fountain of blood gushing. I am in our house, in the room I sleep in. The bed sheets are stark white, starched and crisp. Throughout the slaughter of the pig, I cover my head with the pillow and press it hard against my ears, to no avail. The squeals make me shiver. I pound my head against the bed and the sound of old springs detract from the noise in the yard. After silence, after death, the pool of warm blood presides.

When it is over, the covers come off, I step outside and smell the cauldron in the backyard. The stench of prey, the apron wet with splotches of blood.

"Who wants the ears?" he yells, seeing me approach reticently. He chops them off the head that is in his arms. Then, he throws them in the boiling water. We fight over the ears and who'd have most of the crunchy pig skin. Sometimes we spit out the hair and say:

"Ewwww", with our eyes. All smiles when our mouths are full of pigskin and our bellies getting fed.

Dedi And The Neighbor

I am hungry to hear of it, but fearful of what I am about to uncover. They complain about the red headed neighbor, who sits at her window sill and does not feed her grandchildren when they are hungry. I know, I play with them. He knows, because grandpa is sleeping with her behind Buni's back. I find out when I enter the bedroom of the house one afternoon after school and I see them in bed. The red headed grandmother smoking, her generous curls over her big breasts, that burst out of her white bra. Grandpa looks at me, and I cannot remember an ounce of regret in his expression. I am eight. I run out and the hallway seems longer than usual, I trip over the threshold and do not eat dinner that night. I sob silently and steal a cigarette from grandma's spare purse. At Vali's house, down the block, I run with him to the back of the garden, we kneel and puff away. I love grandpa, I love grandma too, but I adore him. I punch a few more boys that week and assert myself as the tomboy on the block. No one can outrun me. I speed through the school yard and hide behind the gym, where I tell stories about the uncle who lives in America.

Hungry?

The clover green gate slams. I hear shuffling of feet on the ground. The wheels of Dedi's bike turned with a rusty chain around them. He is home from the butcher shop. The black leather case is filled with, shhhhhh…… I want to tell you a secret. After we eat what is in the case, the sausage and cheese, the black bread, then he calls me over to him. I sit on his lap. My seven-year-old body is frail, my stomach concave, my protruding collar bones are not the only bones visible, easily breakable, sharp like knives, through my olive translucent skin. He holds me close to his reddened face, from the vodka, the work, the sun, the rage. The blue eyes flicker above the bags under his eyes. I am still. I count the spots of yellow inside his irises. The right hand, the dominant, precise slasher, rubs my belly. He rubs, looks up at me and says: "My light, my sunshine, did you have enough to eat? Are you full? Look at Dedi, tell me Adela." His leg lifts. My body shifts on the other leg. He rubs. He is not cutting any throats. His fist is not pounding on the table. I am not still. I sit looking at Dedi, while my body is meeting his hand. The hand that takes lives, cuts the food, feeds me. I can see the wife-beater on him stained with brown dry blood, the rows of thread interrupted by holes, the air tinged with his sweat.

Topogan

    At Dedi's butcher shop, after the slaughter on the first floor, the meat makes its way down to the basement. The butchers clean and insert it through fireplace openings. The animal slides down to the room with the oversized scales. The men hang the slabs on ceiling hooks in the gigantic fridge. Sounds cannot be heard through the fridge doors—

          my brother and I play

          hide and squeak

          screaming in our uniforms

          we jump through

          the opening

          onto the bloody slide

          the needle points

          frantically

          right, both of us

          on the scale, laughter

          until one of us

          slips away.

Dedi's Absence

I look at the old photo album and see a baby picture. My gaze gets foggy and my mind wonders. Our houses were strung along like pearls on a necklace tied together, yet separate, similar, yet not the same. I see her now, the neighbor who had no children, or they were grown and gone. I was not a teenager yet and played doctor without shame with friends. We were his grandchildren. We were his flesh and blood, for who knows much about mom's side of the family? Honoring him was our priority. We were not his. What I am trying to say here is the truth unfiltered. One morning, playing in grandma's absence in the garden, grandma was visiting my Uncle in the US. My footsteps rushed to grandpa's house, I was hungry and sweaty, I wanted the coolness of the house.
I wanted him to make me fried toast and I wanted him to douse it in paprika. Except I did not know, how could I? I rushed through the long corridor that separated the kitchen from the bedrooms.

Streams of afternoon light poured through the curtains. His bedroom door was cracked open. I pushed on the glass part of the door, and there I saw in grandma's side of the bed, the neighbor lady with her cleavage out smoking a cigarette next to my grandpa.

I felt it all in my chest—a steady pounding, part warning, part hunger.

Nothing could have prepared me for this moment. If parents and grandparents take vows towards each other, then what about the children? The promise to protect them from themselves. Their worst selves that push through the toughest of times. The ugliness of parents and grandparents is seldom spoken of. I am the rebel that I am today, for I am in complete reactionary mode against them. I am a composite of reactions towards my caretakers.

Buni's Silence

The cat got her tongue, silent like a baby sleeping, or a cup of water sitting on the table. A ticket for the metro in Paris, without any holes because you did not travel anywhere just yet. She was silent as if the cat cut her tongue. She was silent as a feather falling from the roof to the street. The light struck her sometimes from an angle and lit up her eyes, but the rest of her face seemed harsh, her lips were taught and miserly. If she loved you dearly you'd know it. She forbade her grandkids to come visit because her husband was tired and needed to rest. We, the grandkids, were starving and he was the food provider for the entire family. What could we do? We begged her to make us fried potatoes, if there was no meat. She refused. One time when I held my toothbrush to receive toothpaste, grandma squeezed the tube so hard that the toothpaste splattered in my eyes. I cried so hard I recall the pain to this day. But this is not the story I have started here. She was misunderstood. Her name was Ileana Wilhelmina. In the kitchen she would sit in the corner by the stove and have her Carpati cigarettes, and Nescafe, each morning without fail. There was a cloud of smoke surrounding her out of sorts coiffed hair. She dyed her hair dark brown till late in her life. When she smiled, it made us smile. We ran around outside for hours, then at lunch, she'd call us to come in and eat. We sat down at the table, covered in a red and white checkered linoleum tablecloth. She was behind and beside us, saying nothing at all, preparing the next course of the meal. A breeze. An unnoticeable part of an ensemble chorus that would sing beautifully as a unit, yet all the separate cogs did not make sense solo. Grandma Wilhelmina, Buni Iluș, was a hairdresser and gave perms to all the neighbors in our kitchen. The smells of the fumes from the rollers and the dyes were noxious. I get a headache thinking about the smells. When it came to favoring a son, she did and it was not my father whom she favored. The benefit of being a favorite made the favorite run away from home in the 70s never to look back to where he came from ever again. There is not much to the story, except I would like to have understood her silences. I do not know how else to describe her goodness, I do not know if there was some. I do not know how to speak of her because she herself did not speak. Both my father and I are extremely expressive mammals. We speak, we cry out, we protest with words, we gesture with our hands. She did none of that. What if she did not love her husband? Her eldest boy. Me for that matter, my brother? The golden child fled the nest.

What was left for her from the family pie? Was she a loner because she was so heartbroken? The silence she emanated haunts me to this day. It bores into me like the color blue, emanates from mother's paintbrush onto the wet canvas.

River of blues and shades of painful memories.

In The Beginning

I begged to stay in. I never wanted to know her love. It complicated the game of cat and mouse. I was in the basement of my soul with a gut full of feelings towards her. I tried to forgive her for eating cherries and strawberries. I became allergic to seafood and mushrooms later in my life. Who are you allergic to?

Choking, I come to you. You put your sweaty palm on the nape of my neck and say, *"Oh come on, come on, you will be alright. You love me, right?"* I cannot absorb your heart inside mine. I cannot absolve us of our sins. Palpitations. Functional murmurs. Maybe I was always a beat behind. Heart irritations. The acid reflux could have killed me but it just gave me warning after warning, then left me breathless.

My illness

brings out the mother in me

      the animal

fighting for life

at any price

I did not imagine

the body you tamed

      would turn savage

My will is gone, it left

only animal.

Our House

This is what happened: it was a long time ago. The house was dark and shuttered. I did not go back except once, 27 years ago, a miracle of the cold snow. I slipped away, but not before the callous weather withered my hands. I thought I would die. I said to myself, open your eyes. But not before you open your hands. Life to life. Death to the end of another life. Life until death. The cold green gate opened slowly. Miracle of the soft snow. There is nothing I am omitting here, just leaving you out like a polar bear in the Arctic on your floating icy island. Don't hold me responsible for the omissions of my heart. Should you need me, call upon me. To the black walls, with the white lettered writing. If I could tattoo my soul, I would use red ink. The house was dark and shuttered. She shut the doors before entering the corridor. What scares me is the only thing I would risk dying for. A strange miracle saved her. She is me. Fully in her fervent hands, I moved and shifted my body. Into the sands in the valley of the mountains, the snow peaks, the winds from the West, that came in to sweep, into the sands I fell that poured in waves and reddened the air with smoke. I will come back, I whispered. To what, though? I kissed her with all the life in me, life to life, warm enough to lift her. Opening like a paycheck, like an estate overlooking a large lake. Miracle of holding her in my hand. I gave myself through my hand, walking hand in hand in the village, under a poplar tree? Or was it an American Elm? We walked into the house that was shuttered and dark. Dank, damp, dainty. We walked, our lives depended on it. Life to life, betrayed the ones that made up my life prior to her. Hand in hand in the dark to forget. The weather did not interfere with us. My fervent hands, we stopped in for tea. Maybe I bought Kombucha, we held the cold bottle in our hands. Only the living could die, you said. The fungus in the Kombucha was still alive, I could feel its fervent nature inside my stomach. I thought she would die. She just dropped my hand, the grip that held it all together. I did not go back to Saint Mark's Church on the corner, outside the organic market near 8th street. I just remembered kissing her with all the life in me. The dark and disinterested night left me too. All the stars are not just ours anymore. The black alley cat on the glassy sidewalk, alone among the frost-cast stars.

They found me, sprawled on the pavement, in the tiny sonorous, echo-bound courtyard. The houses around were dark and shuttered. I can only die if I was ever alive, I died at 23, right before I met her. A hungry ghost. A displaced entity. Conceived in the dark, under the stars. The fabric of their union still haunts me. I left my body at 23, walking a narrow street towards home, when the Reaper came. I flew from my own body into the stars and touched the universe where there was no longer an atmosphere. Weightless fleck of dust. To breathe was no longer necessary. I do not remember leaving space. Or how the earth caught me in my whirling wheels of pain.

Did I see her again? Or did I suffer from retinitis pigmentosa? There were colors buried in the blaze of white, and a fragile ghost of a being, dressed like it had forgotten who it was. Did I see her again? On a ledge in the city at night?

It was not the wings that lifted me, nor broke my fall, when I had landed again back on earth. Who bound me? I looked in the curls of women's hair, the eyes of passersby. I thought she had died. But, it was me. This in-between is where I found the single cell model of my life. Still alive.

Was I alone? I looked up.

Circle Of The Sun

Light spilled in. It emptied the dark from the room. Corners glowed like a hymn. She turned her back to the heat. Let it climb her spine. Opened the window. The light crowned her. She burned. The fire touched her lips. She bit down on it—a thin coin of gold. For a breath, she looked lit from within. Like something holy.

She opened her back to the sun and let it heat her spine. Each tendril and each vertebrae moved, embraced by the warmth. Honey, viscous and amber slipped down towards the base. A red sparrow waiting for night, lightness in her flight. She did not intuit what was going on outside herself. It was too delicious inside.

She had the sun by her side. The circling of fire and orange liquid warmth was all she needed to form a cocoon. What came out surprised all. Flies gathered at the length of her back and sat still as if their thin legs were stuck in molasses. They waited, she waited, we all waited. Until the sun set. We could see more of her without all the halos around her face and head. Be spontaneous, she thought. Come out of the shell that broke long before you were born. Forget the failures early in life. Look at all the lauded winners, who have audiences applauding them by the hundreds. She wanted to feel the independence of having performed the greatest thing ever, knowing she was never awarded the tools for this task. She knew they would come and gather, and further her strength by their numbers. Her audience was ooooooooohing and ahhhhhhhing near and far. She covered them in the honey of her light. They praised the warmth of the words that dripped out of her mouth. A baby knows when her mother is happy or sad. They all knew her and lived near her breath in order to take in more of the glow.

This Is How I Ran Away At Seven

I could not afford her. Her hands cross in front of her. She is losing her child. I need to know when there is a window. I cross my arms by the Mureş River. I smile without acknowledging what I know. There is a road.

The road crosses the Mureş River, paved upon the feet of the bridge. I stand there at a crossroads. She calls me home. I smile to show how far my mouth stretches. How tiny and separate my teeth are. Decisive audiences always participate.

 Through the gap.

We are rivers   apart.

I Grew And Grew At Nine, I Was As Tall As I Would Be In Adulthood

She protected herself against herself.
She talked.
The story clung to me.
Wove itself through my hair.
Nestled in the dark corners of my head.
I couldn't shake it loose.
What constricted me is other dead women's clothes—and too-tight-fitting clothes that no longer suit me. Why do I have to be so big in waiting? What is gestating inside me? I am round, shapely, and unapologetically fierce. I am curved like an hourglass that men look at and want to rub like a genie bottle.

> One day I will escape from *the slings and arrows of my misfortune.*

If you were to come mama or dad to tell me how I should count my blessings then come.

I stepped into the red room.
Not the first room. But the one that stayed.
I moved toward what's next.
Saw something coming.

Couldn't name it.
Still can't.
Smell the roses, you tell me after lunch. I am not full on this day.

I dreamt of Rose on my shoulders as I carried her to the day camp where she was supposed to play. I cannot name this future—it feels like a pregnancy. In gestation, I suffer from growth. There was no time for Eva Hesse. Headaches pushed against her tumor in her brain. The pain pushed inside the strings in her sculptures. So what if these are not all my words.

I lullabied my way to sleep last night. Today, I ate my way into oblivion. When I eat I do not feel the ache. Little by little, what is killing me is saving me. Or is it? I have waited for my own story to ripen to an ending. I did not find the resoluteness inside myself to save myself then.

The most well-thought of Saints erased violence without retaliation. I am going to yell into my pillow and yellow my nightgown. Let the stream stain me.

My lover found me in what is not revealed. I sleep in the white cotton nightgown, down to my ankles. He reveled in strategically exposed skin, kissed this and that of me. Spent time kissing my forehead—more than my parents kissed me there as I was growing up. They want me to count my blessings. I must punish them for their crude reality. When things hurt they hurt all of us. Gaming with only their own terms for memories to show up at my party is just not fair.

I don't know myself as much as I know my shame.

I have lived with it for as long as I can remember having a first memory. The game is up—cat and mouse—I am both and the punishment always falls on my lap. The self-flagellator must go away to come back another day. To calibrate revenge: sing *"ring-around-the-rosy"* so many times.

We used to play hopscotch. Jumping up and down inside numbered squares left a mark on me. I still want to stand still and jump inside the definition of safe. Do not pretend you did not hear my cry for help. I yell inside pillows until my bladder explodes. Call it quits when my temples are pulsing with verve.

I cannot fathom how men eat up damage.

When I watched Juliette Binoche in the role of the painter, I squinted at the screen and saw my mother. She does not know just how damaged I am. I took residence a floor below my mother. Too close for comfort yet further than the smell of her perfume.

There is something that betrayed me. I am not free. I left my home to go into the nether regions of Queens on a cold and rainy day in search of a birthday *gateau*. It was a terrible decision and my body did not listen.

I ate as if food would be gone forever.
I never knew this kind of hunger   until now.

Listen, I do not carry any resemblance to a mother. I carry the shame of having had the chance in this lifetime with the mire that comes with manhood.

We are meant to carry each other into the night.

Marlon James listens to War Music before he starts writing his novels. Before I write, I listen to Jeannette Winterson's words. I want a do-over. If listening were this: sitting and opening. The *ghiocei* (snowdrops) in Central Park are one life and they are not the same. What will prompt me to allow my own Spring to come forth? For me to blossom in full glory? Quieting every sense.

In the slowness of molasses I can find the answers: yearning, calling, birds singing, the smell of roses. A preposition dangling at the end of a sentence I try to convey meaning with.

I Left My House

left this morning.
Didn't feel like turning back.
They were there.
I was not.
I stared at the building—
just another face in a row of blank faces.
I've never really lived inside.
The version of me they saw—
a shadow at best.
I move quietly.
Half-there.
Something between breath and silence.
The light is gone.
And I'm still here.
Waiting for something to shift.
To start.

    I left behind the couch, not the loveseat. I do not have a loveseat. At the seat of my love you are bound in chains. Scratch that. I am bound to the seat of your love instead.
    I already love you, but I do not tell you. I tell of this and that of you, I name parts, never reveal how I feel about them. You make the melting process the one I want to be a part of. You melt with me, inside me, beside me. Always above, behind and besides me.

spoon

(after "The Wooden Spoon")

object—
 not quite arm
 not quite god

                                                breath

                                                in the narrow room

 a smear
 a glare

                                                no swallow

 a room
 dimmed
 by flame

                                                her face
                                              ticks—
                                              not time

 outside
 a laugh

 inside—
 a hush
 a held breath

                                              wooden
                                                intent
                                               not touch

I shift
stay still

                                               flicker

                     shadows stretch
bread lingers

my hand
curves inward
like a question

                                              I forge
                                              the moment

only
this pulse
remains

                                              waiting

Mama's Green Bike

Communists steal the bicycle seat from mama's green bike. They leave the rod, pointing upward, rusted and menacing. This is how they fuck her.

She makes sure to hop on and rapidly ride away, not sitting but standing, raising her behind in order not to fall on their phallic weapon. The phone tapped, and all conversations reported, being followed by them makes mama transparent, a traitor and a target. This is how they rape her.

She rides on cobble-stoned streets to Dedi's house where we live. If she escapes this time, she gets to speak on the phone to Dad. The conversation is taped, studied and minced. Her deformed bike makes her work hard at keeping alive.

Unbeknownst to her, until the age of 13, mama is adopted.
This is how her parents do not want her.

As a two year old, she is in a dingy, moldy room in a crib, on a divan bed, on the floor on a down comforter. No eyes watching her. No mother's hands changing her diapers. No lactating breasts.

>Milk and honey do not flow.

In fact, her arthritic hands now hurt when she is painting the country road scene with pastels. *"Why do my bones hurt so much? I cannot even finish my painting today."* Mama I know why, please can I tell you?

>Mama's bones do not develop.

Dad's Ways

By 6, I know what he needs. He is an orphan. I see his tired body on the sofa. I know the springs and the sound each makes when he lays on his side, curled in a fetal position. I place the red blanket on his body to his chin, carefully, tuck it into the crevices of the sofa. I start at his upper back and move down around his feet. He takes off his shoes this time. The shins, his stomach. His arms are bent. I know each finger so well. Exposed, I do not cover them. I start the ritual, take his thumb in my hand, squeeze gently and roll it. When I reach the tip, I press my nail in. He has performed the ritual on me. It is how I learned about him. I always allow the pinch of his nail on my fingertips to feel like pleasure. I memorize how he touches my hands. The mirror is funny these days. Dad with striking blue eyes. A map of erosions. He stamps my passport when I enter his country. Ours.

The language of our country had no boundaries.

I am with my brother Alex at Marcel's house. I am eight-years-old. The boys are two years younger. Marcel's mother has short hair, looks German and smells French. Later I realized her perfume was Mademoiselle by Chanel. She works at Customs, where she procures toys for her son. We are sitting on the living room floor. The boys are busy with cars. Alex loves coming. I get bored. Why today? Nothing special happens.

I cannot hear any noise. I do not notice her coiffe out of place when she returns to the living room, after being absent for some time. Did they go to the kitchen? Maybe they stayed there a bit too long.

At 13, mom reveals my father's infidelities. She confides in me from her bedroom in 540 Main Street, apartment 1022. I am in the doorway, trying to walk away. I go back, in my mind, to that day at Marcel's house. I know in every fiber of my being it is true. My obsession begins with the blond mother, her hair perfectly in place by the power of hairspray, 80s style. I observe her. In summer, I walk by her beach towel. I want to smell her. The Mademoiselle by Chanel, the coconut sunscreen, the minty gum and cigarette. This is how close I want to be.

Hansel & Gretel

The dynamics of disappearing. Crumb by crumb, fragments are dropped in the woods. The green beyond and last night I dream of money. Crumb by crumb, fragments are scattered. The book. The boy. The body. The love. The life. My inventions. I am a boy. I am here and gone the next moment. The result of falling out of love with Rebecca and Ioana. I wonder if the missing will translate into taking steps. I am a boy. Forgotten. Gorgeous on the inside. Externally, I am a girl. Come, judge. You cannot fathom further than my presentation. I present well. I seduce you on the page. The pacing of something that needs to come out, despite itself and the owner of its invention. I am a writer. A director of diction, vernacular, special sovereignty to save me. In my poesie I am chasing the blues. Inviting the dark from beyond into the crushed paper of my heart. I am here to stay with you if you choose me. I am a boy. I have never forgotten how to make this go away. A fact. A body. An impostor. I sit in the audience at the poetry reading and listen to the boys read their woes. I am a poet. You stomach only parts of the scent I emanate. I am flower, gardenia and water lilies. I am a boy. Covered in truth. Are you going to follow? Not all the fragments return. I am filled with love. Broken like a crazy town after the devastation of a tornado. I am supposed to pump out writing.

I watched him kill the stray dog with the open door of the car while we flew on the road at high speed. The German Shepherd fell to the ground. We got melted ice-cream to go. Or was it the time the ambulance banged into the biker and killed him on the spot? I am a boy. I am here to stay. Did the dog die? I saw him fall flat to cobblestones soaked in his blood. Hallelujah. May the carnage stop someday. May I give up meat for good.

I want to tell you a story of when I punched and kicked to get out and when I came out, they said look at her, she is a boy. My hands used to play piano. I am in Arad, Romania. My fingers caress the keys in Chopin, sometimes Bach. I glide like Lavinia. She is my best friend.

We met on the steps leading up to her house. If you turn into the living room door you can see the grand piano. I played for hours some days. Other days, she played. Anyways, through the large French windows of the living room would come out the sounds of classical music. The wind was afraid to drown us out, and the leaves did not blow through the window, but we could feel the leaves swirling deciding their next note. We were kind of invincible. Best friends in no time, because we could piece the world together. If I were a boy, I would love myself hard. Some oblivion is necessary to believe in inventions. Come closer. Help me pick up the crumbs. The audience is hungry. Thursday you will go see a play on Broadway. You pay to have someone else pick up the pieces, make sense of fragments, lapses of memory and make you go on your way uplifted. I am not feeling this now. I do not care. I am getting to the bottom of this page and I will leave you. You will not make a prisoner out of me. I will not have you testify in my defense. I have wronged you. Most importantly I have wronged myself. I am a boy, right?

What was I saying? This is the most I will digress in one chapter before I call it quits. It is not a competition. I am not a winner. I am a poet. I am a boy. The allergy pushes the sneezes out explosively, extolling that which does not agree with you. You are allergic to yourself. Peace comes to those who accept. Radical acceptance. I do not accept acceptance. I would like to take back the crumbs from the Hansel & Gretel woods of my memory, pick them off from ferns and dirt, look at them in the palm of my hand and gobble them quickly. I want the hand that rocks the cradle to reach out to me and rock me. Leave the butcher's knife and the wooden spoon. Maybe then I can face you and maybe then I can face this. I am a boy.

Reins Of Time And Dust

For the moment, the action stopped. The fantasy started and we left. Went outside ourselves in order not to lie and carry burdens out loud in the light of day. I want to tell you about it. He was staring me down at the bar, in Battery Park City. I was with Love in front of me, in my lap. Love always held me close to its bosom. I did not flinch, nor move my eyes away from Love towards blame and woe. I withstood the test of time from a distance. My eyes rested tempestuously on Love as they should have. With Love, we make all kinds of good things. I make crowns with philosophical treatise dangling as fringes from the sides. I invent what inventing means and feels like. Electricity in my mind! Shockwaves of joy! Absorbed inside my bloodstream I take Love into my veins, relinquishing the reins of time and dust. To be able to be real you must not exist. You know what I mean. I was talking to Fantasy and wanted to take it to the next level. I was alright in the timeline and the weight I carried around each day inside my pocket book. I call it the backpack. When you disappear I reenter the room like a Queen. I am woeful. I am wistful. I am right. In this state of Grace, my cheeks are not flushed. My skin is pale, inviting to shadows, as I walk the marble floor down the mirrored hall. I do not want to make sense. I get deeper into Fantasy and their voices bounce and abound with nonsense and non-essence. The mirrors' reflections are full of temporal distortions.

I loved once before and now I am impeding Love from loving me. I am an obstacle course that must course through me for success in the reality of time. I want a deeper story. I want Fantasy to take me down, abysmally down, from where I could never escape nor turn around and come back the same. I drink blood. I take the reins and lead. I am here in the historical hallway where heads are bowed with obeissance. I love the frankness with which I waltz. Water drips heavily on the walls and reflects in mirrors, I wait. I wait for you among loud voices. I wait for you in the dimly lit hallway. At this rate, I will drown before you come. So why don't you just come?

As soon as we bought the apartment our living room doubled. We were sitting on our orange plush L-shaped couch, all the walls expanded, moved outward to leave us in the middle of space. This is how we grew out of misery. We wanted to be exposed, watched and listened to. Finally, an audience for our conundrum. The audience is hungry for the shenanigans. We were blamed for being up all this time. We grew invincible. If I were to describe the experience I would begin with its feeling. A childless woman in her late 40s.

the sea that recedes
always
finds its shore

The animal came first. The echoes of a life about to be lost. The bouncing of the squeals off the walls of our humiliating house.

When I lived on a mountain I could see the villagers running in ceremony to the ceremony in which they sacrifice the animal. On this day in April, I arrived first. The yells were a distant echo of the lives below. One less well lived life would continue today. The sow is their sacrifice.

I dispel the magic cast upon their lives, the dark matter that continues in the crevices of their souls. This is all they knew. Their lives were a sanctimonious sanatorium of the things they never knew. I wanted to say the things they have lost. Although, they never possessed them in the first place.

The smoker is ready for the slabs of meat. The incisions are extremely precise under the leadership of Dedi, who is a stellar butcher. He is solicited by all the cultural groups living in Pârneava, our neighborhood. He cuts for each of these groups. Busy all days of the week and sometimes the carnage lives inside the weekends. Or dies, depending on how you see it.

I Sent My Courage To The Moon

        The thin line between knowing and not knowing.

Craters welcome me. The atmosphere didn't.

Gravity was kind to me. If I am not bogged down I can jump like an Olympian. Archangels including Michael sing to me. The pain that usually runs through the left side of my body and head is vacuumed into a vortex. I missed hypnosis and my teacher and my students. Bagels too for that matter. Scooped with scallions, cream cheese and paprika.

Nobody was alongside me on the Moon. I missed no-one. Once in a while, kidding under rivulets of thought, Earth formed and bound, and I skipped on at an uninflected pace.

The meditative silence of the Moon, the pure lack of atmosphere, sound waves beyond intent. If I could survive with only intent. Intent to breathe, eat, walk, sleep, drink water. Devoid of doing—Intent to become

        a speck of the Universe.

You carry eternal knowledge, scientific discovery, God, Buddha, human form, energy and pureness. Attention goes where energy flows. There is no need to let go of desire.

I Don't Know How To Write A Story

I can tell a story. Fragmentary moments between lapses. Read and listen. There's a beat. My irreverent heartbeat. Unforgiving. Unoffered. Use for it remains. Replay the tape, skip over damaged areas, return to the unbroken sequence, ripple the stone inside the pond, the contract was broken.

I can repair things that are broken. Honey, I promise I can. I do not know what to do with what has broken since you've gone. The puzzle does not relent. It can't go away until it solves itself. The answer is inside the answer. Inside the union of us. But since there is not a union, I am left in the sand. Trekking the desert without proper gear. Walking on the dunes, never to encounter water. You are my *fata morgana*. I caress the outline of your face. The forgiving beard. The place where I rest my eyes, when your look was too intense. You pick honest berries for breakfast, savor them through evening. I want you to be honest. You were honest. Just not the way I had hoped. Joking aside, it is in your honesty that I grew. It is where I felt alone. Expansive for my body to carry me anymore. When hiding corners have the lights shed on them, they act like pastures for freedom to graze on. I did not know just how much of you I internalized. I had to push you away. I have practice at this. I perfected the method. Fullproofed it. Pulled it out seamlessly. Hit you over the head with it, before you knew what hit you. You took it. I did not expect it. Further and further the story spun out of control. My dishonesty returned like a nomad found my oasis and anchored the ship. Why could you not guide me through the desert? I spoke of damnation, mine. I pressed your heart repeatedly. Tell me STOP. My mouth rambles, my mind spins the story.

I have shocked you senseless. That's what dehydration and delirium do. Fill you with ravaging nonsense. I need you to put out your hand and push me to the well, then pull me into you. Save what I have left. What is pure? What I have for you, is sought after.

My mind used your anger as a ticket for the bus. I felt you sank into the couch, on the corner of Morgan, at Greenpoint Heights. My glass of beer more than half full after three hours of ramble. I could count on your anger. This was my out. The last week. Closest I have been to you. Day in and day out for three days and three nights. Sharing the smallness of your bedroom, in which the bed was principal island to float in. I digress. I am afraid to lose you all over again. To admit to my mistake that broke your heart. Stamped by your doubt in women. I am your passport out of this land. You mistrusted words that wobbled on crutches. I held on for dear life, had been quiet for too long. Silence connected us. The room you made for me remained silent.

With pushed words out of my mouth, I declared love. You stayed silent. In the dark of the bedroom in the Berkshires, you turned to me to kiss me goodnight. I felt a slight touch of your tongue. In stillness it moved. Moved me, to open my mouth wider. I lured you in. Hooked on to life. I thought you were tired. You were inside me instantly. In the morning, during coffee on the porch facing the windmills, I felt us old sitting in silence again. Still touching. This is where you tell me stories. Read to me by the fire. The details are in the objects collected, arranged, burying your characters. Obsessive under the weight of your body, on the gray couch, I sweat but I cannot orgasm. It is one of my deepest fears. Giving up control. I can easily come. Not when I am with another. You are the one who has brought me to tears in this tenderness. Entered me, without words. The natural union.

Nothing is natural when I orgasm. It is a game. Cat and mouse. I run as fast as I can. When I catch myself I can't resist and I crash into waves of pleasure that pinch my prisoner self. Never devoid of pain. It is what I was trying to tell you. Hurt me while you are inside. It is the only way I can reel myself out on the carpet of abandonment. Caressed into submission. Admitting that I am not experienced at sharing my pleasure. Since you did not pain me into pleasure, I detached. You lost interest. Angry at your lack of attraction, I gave you nothing and thought I contributed everything. I could not hide. Naked and sweating lies. The way I breathed and moved gave me away. My heart watched from its chambers as your chest gently pressed onto mine. No opening to let you in. We lasted very long. In my quest to run, yours to catch me. Run after what you deserved. I got lost along the shame and guilt. The heavy weights. You pleasured me. My legs spread out before you. I would have come through, had I not pushed you away. We had tried for months, you were tired. My love was declared verbally, yours needed our bodies.

The more I said I loved you, the more silent you became. The more tender you were, the more withdrawn my body was. I had not seen you in over a week. After a fight and a flu. I planned out the dress. We both wanted to see the midnight show. Our hands reached for erogenous places. Passion pulled our bodies down into one seat. Curtains pulled, disappearing into darkness.

April 12, 2018

I avoid being bruised. He must mean something different.
That shit belongs to him, not me.

When I was growing up I rebelled against feeling and now my feelings rebel against me. They await my arrival.

Something pushes me
           over   the rainbow
    there is a valley
with starving animals.

In The Gut

symmetries of the moon
traverse thresholds
only lovers do. At night

delight discover
a pull.   Move closer
to the edge

pushed into oblivion
by a cloud of dust

through an impending storm—

      or, merely fall

April 11, 2018

She stood at the window. Tracing the fog on the glass. I watched her. I stayed quiet. The kettle began to hiss. A small sound in a house that held so many. She leaned forward, still drawing shapes. I couldn't name them. I didn't ask. I thought: love hides in these small moments. The curve of her back. The crease in her brow. The way her hand hovered, not sure what to erase. I wanted to say something. I didn't. I wanted to keep this. I knew I couldn't.

I shifted in my seat at the kitchen table and obsessed about loss. All the ways I could lose all this preciousness. We knew each other well. Then our eyes locked. I felt the poem that was writing itself inside my mind. I wanted to capture it quickly. Thoughts like feathers began flying in the winds of time. Eventually disappearing into thin air. I made an effort not to look at her with too much expectation. I want the world for her. We get each other. She holds the antidote to loss. I knew it then. I know it now. I could eat all the vegetables in the world. I am healthy only with her. I know why I breathe. She had little to tell me. The snow had not melted outside, as we sat waiting for Spring.

The Prince And The Game

"Forgive me father, for I have fallen."
"Was it the body or the soul?"
"The body."
"Then speak it into light, I am listening."

I am 7, prancing around the house not able to find a good distraction. I am about to find the meaning of patience or something exciting to get me out of myself again. The doorbell rings. It is my friend from class. We are in 5th grade together at Școala Generală no. 4. Our teacher is buried into the weekend to be resurrected in two days' time. Mara walks into the discovery zone. I do not recall what smelled more bitter and sour at the same time, the day old coffee in the kitchen of my dad's forgetfulness, or Mara's clothes imbued with basement mold and cooked schnitzel from her mother's kitchen. Here we are, together in an adult-less world. Our parents are somewhere at the Alimentara forming lines for bread, then more lines for butter, and the longest line they stand in for is meat. This goes on for hours. For us. For our mouths to be fed. Our bellies not to grumble.

Mara is uncouth. Mousy colored hair in all directions, while mine is black, silky and smooth. Long down my back to my waist. I invite her to sit.

"Do you want water?" No. Let's listen to some music. Ohhh, wait, the electricity is cut. "Let's play a game." Have you read the story of the princess and her long hair that she dropped from the balcony for the prince to climb and reach her? Save her!

I want to save us from the mundane.

I tell Mara she is the princess. Because we are alone and because I am a good friend, I will be the prince. I will save us both from the world of lines

                                            dirty starched linens

heavy feather down comforters that weigh us down into oblivion at night.

      I tell Mara that I have a comb and mirror for her to comb her hair. I am direct. Not recycling any storylines but inventing new ones as we go. After the brushing of her hair, I tell Mara she should lay down over the comforter, pink and cold and soft.

"Rest until the prince will come to save you. I will climb up to the window of your room. Wait for me. Close your eyes. When I make it into the room you will know. You will feel me."

She not only listened, but she was relaxed and comfortable. Smiling and expectant. I make as little noise as possible as I climb to Mara's window. I make it to the top and enter through the window to save her. She is sleeping on the bed in her small room. I reach the bed. Look from my vantage point at Mara, as she waits for me. The game continues.

My body leads me to lie down next to her as her lids open. She laughs as my breath warms her neck. I start to climb her waist with one leg until I am straddling her. I lean down to her face, tell her the prince will kiss her now. The prince is so happy to rescue Mara. She smiles. I bend down, we kiss. My body on top of hers. Her eyes flutter open, but neither of us speaks. The prince has come and gone, leaving behind a silence
too heavy for children to carry.

"Father, I have sinned."

Yearning For Light

We wanted light. Not sunlight, but something else. Something seamless that moved through us without asking. It touched the forehead like a thought, then vanished. It didn't come once. It returned, again and again, but never in the same way. A shimmering ocean in the early, early hours. Not singular, but layered. When it touched us, it didn't warm—it opened. It carved us open. Something inside gave way. Something stayed behind.

I had found an old Confessional Box. Hungarian wood and splintered. I stumbled like a cripple over the memory inside the Church in Budapest. Laying in the pewters, taking an afternoon nap, noticing sunlight streaming through the humble clothes of Mary holding Jesus in mural-vibrant colors. While my body rested, they gathered. In their Sunday best. It was Wednesday afternoon. A lost day. Rumors were rising inside the Church walls. Was there a Priest among them? Confessing or digesting. The choral of whispers, under the light post-rain sun. I raised an eyebrow. My hand brushed drool from the corner of my mouth. I pulled myself up halfway up in the pewter. Looking for a priest or confessing. All I saw at the back of the Church was the door.

If They Smile, Kiss Them For Me

Kiss them for me by Siouxsie and the Banshees, plays in my mind.

Her mother's beak came toward her. She clipped her wings and learned to keep them by her side. Inspired, without letting anyone know. This was her offense against the world. Secrets twitch under feathers. Her heart beat more intensely. She wanted to show her bruises to the ones who could not see or listen. Her face became a dirt yard where hens pecked. She wanted the truth to long for her. Come on, smile. Truth was abounding, an ache inside her chest. Like the pit of a ripe walnut, a jewel ready to be worn in public.

Her mother's face was close.
"Why don't you smile like the others?"
She tried—but her mouth stayed quiet.
At   night,   a   kiss   that   missed.
A   tap.
 A test.
"Come on," her mother said, "Let me see it."
But the smile was hiding somewhere deep.

Under mother's firm hand, the gap at the front of her teeth showed. This was the best she could pluck up. The price was high for pleasing her mother. Plucked with bare skin exposed, she remained as such for the next 30 years.

Her   mother   lives   above   her.
A   hum   in   the   ceiling.
 A shadow that stays.
No   one   keeps   the   tally   now.
The days drift.
She   shapes   herself
                                    into   light,
into   yes,
into   almost.
A   smile   pulled   from   somewhere   deep—

measured,
mended,
offered.

One night, she moved through the hours like a sacrifice. One night, she martyred her way through time. Then, she stopped.

She looked at her reflection. For once, her face was only her own. No trace of her mother's mouth. No shadow of her father's eyes. The hour had come.

Why didn't she smile like other girls? Because she only recently learned the meaning of freedom.

The meaning of freedom
black and blue　　　　invisible
　　　　　　　　　　　　bruises—honey
colored eyes shine
　　　　　　　　　　under neon lights
　　　　　　　　　　scream
until you belly laugh
　　　　　　　　　　years will pass
before you. Look
in the mirror　　　　at the woman,
you've become.

I Cannot Lie—~~The Corrections~~

As if each step led me to this station. Stationary in a space in time, void of meaning. Full of life and meaning. As if everything that happened before this was a different kind of script and I, a solitary actress. Puppeteered by devices long in place before my consciousness could take hold. Mechanically riding the bull, yet knowing I'd fall off each time in a safe place. Deeper than the one before it, closer to pain and denial. What do I want? Unwritten, I do not know. Unscripted, I cannot follow. Dauntingly haunted by the characters of old, I awkwardly let tears fall. As if my soothing song of bedtime is an awful sting of a feeling, coming from what I'm hearing. I always want to not hear what I am hearing. As if I have left a piece of me in each lie told. As if truth was a current that came around my house once every ten years and swept me far away from the shore. Is there a lighthouse where I can find a home? A functioning door that can close out the waves? A light that can beckon me into being alive? Alive in the sense of feeling everything, putting it down in words and sharing it. Even if I am the audience, when I am the sole audience, I must stop the muttering and muster up the courage to sit tightly to listen. As if listening was at the end of the beginning of the world for myself. As if this rush of blood to the head, trying to numb me with its pain and threatening consequence, unconsciousness, would not succeed. As if the place to speak from is the most consequential and current feeling I've ever lived and inhabited. As if the more I inhabit my feeling of now, I could demand the answers to lead me to myself. The questions can form and take shape and make me shapely in their abundance. The circulation on the streets of my consciousness can be terribly crowded, yet all roads lead in time to the place. The place of truth. As if fear were a road block, a detour, yet, the map is overcrowded with potential and less concerned with the timing of it all. If in the end, it is the end that causes the beginning, then it would have served its purpose. A means to a start in life. Afterlife even. Only in thorough thoughts can the process take hold. As if anything ever thought of as having consequence is held in the place where tiredness takes over fear and the real unfolding can finally take place. As if thoughts of any kind with so much clarity and light upon them, cannot measure up to the nebulous thinking that surreptitiously seduces with its manic pulse to push through to the other side. Not from exhaustion, but from the exhausting of permutations inside the lie. The big fat lie of hope. If the only real currency were a threat, one upon another, threats to your process, to you, to your consciousness, your awakened soul, then threats will expire soon. Not before they gang up in a ball of fire that tries to annihilate any type of self preservation. If I were a preservationist I would have died long ago. It is in the unpredictability of variables that change the course, in the short lived life of possibilities where hope dies. Where life no longer procreates. Where you no longer are reborn. Where no pulse can restore its own beat to the cadence of an animal. In being erased indirectly by my own selves, I get to a place of recognition of what is not real. Only through a complete disappearance am I able to fathom up the self that breeds in the dark, dank planes of despair. Right along with the poetics of discovery in there lies the actual person I am. The pain of reading something I should have written, is the pain of having been surpassed into birth by the living. As if I was reserved this place of constant reminder of death, the imminence of which is threatening to others, jolts them into living.

For me, the effect is the amount of death I've already lived. With the verve of someone alive I have been buried inside the mind, the heart and organs. Their secretions are constant bitter reminders to my palate that something remains undigested and courses through me raw, unfurled, unfiltered and uncompromising. As if the meal I've been feasting on to maintain this huge proportion and distance I've mustered is the exact cause of my poisoning. The comfort I get from the belly they trace with their eyes on the F train in the mornings I forget to cover up, is that I am in the process of birthing. Rosemary's baby terrifies to the core, due to its vile rejection of the mother towards her baby. The most violent recourse of the rejection is that evil took on my body early on and has been having a field day with me ever since. I cannot object to those I reject with so much volatility. The creases of my brow penetrate deep into my forehead, as if I were conquering my own darkness, pushing it back out into the world, without imposing the real crime. I felt dead inside this afternoon, like a dead silence. The way I am not visible to the naked eye, I am not able to fend off my anger when I am attacked. Its invisible power of taking over images from where they are stored and casting in front of me their horror in instances of out-of-breath definitions from others that do not fit, is a deadening paralysis of my power. In direct proportion of the way I am, is the way I attract those who compose me the way I am not. I love them the most. Out of the world, those to whom I am most devoted emotionally, are the breakers of my spirit. They are my morality, ambition, intellect, kindness, dexterity and passion. For I leave crumbs to myself after having let them fatten the lie. What do I lie about? Everything. As if everything was a bacterial infection that could kill me. And it can. It will. Soon my time in this unsafe zone will expire due to the conflict of interest in my audience. Some attentive as fuck, as much as greedy vultures. The more death abounds inside my marrow, the more their beaks crack the glass that separates. No fear is more of a composite of all fears acting inside me at once, as is their inattention to details. As if they were to look away I would steal a moment in which I had no action. No consequence, but a sheer will to be. As I would be now.

No Witness Will Ever Read This

I've been in training for acceptance, reconciliation, prayer, attunement. You fight. I take flight. My modality is not yours, prayer. I have made a big decision. An incision in my vein to bleed through you. All I did was memorize you. From birth. Rim the edge of the rink with time. My time inside you was not well spent. Yes, I don't know. I have been training in attunement. A screeching violin. Deafening.

Listen—
                              each   drop
                                  a   flicker
  a small pulse of light.
Names   rise
then   vanish
  before they're spoken.

Unmasked Truth

Myopia *my-stress* of error and worry. I misspell mistress and I want to be yours, the one who you lose sleep over. The one who puts you in agony. The one whom you'd give your life. To live you must see. Or be blind. Never in myopia. Truths unmask. The veil between you and the woman you are. In recent crosses with memory's paths, you did not know how to become yourself.

What I know now, I know at 13. It's been a work in verifying. I tried to verify at 23. At the cost of my mind. I reached Nirvana, only to fall deep into hell. I survived because I could not believe my eyes. Myopia of spirit. To protect the spirit. I knew all of its many nuances. Fucking permutations. You can fuck yourself up by believing what you're seeing. This is why I am myopic. By choice. A dance with light, milky and moving, across pupils and iris. Grace shadows. I know what is good and who wants my soul broken. I did not know I'd become a medium for the evils of my youth. Hospitality is part of my nature. Visitors always welcomed—*Chez Adela*. I walked with their horrors, they pulled the black curtains on passenger's lives. Each of you had your white painted over in tar, black dripped out of your sockets and burned the rectus that held your eyeballs in place. You know that I know it. Inhabited the tendons of my body.

My cellular memory is not giving up the brutalities against animals, against the animal that is me. You've undergone mitosis, so my children can remember. You fucker! You plague. I could not contain my poison, it infected my family. Nothing is ever mine.

My body learned early it was public property. The heart, like a fool, gushed. The mind followed. When I started with nothing I had nothing to lose. I want to be your mistress. I want to distress your sleep and steal what was never mine and not yours either. My love, our pain patterns perfectly match—our DNA combined creates a lovebomb. I remain by your silence. You've reduced me to a doctor without her black bag of tricks. Its red lining, all the scalpels and knives needed for me to cut the chords. In silence we are perfect. Oh God, I was tired of your blessings, your supervision, my lack of vision. Battered as I had been at home. Demented recognition. Consuming entanglements. Each time you wobbled away on the crowded subway, my gaze was the laser that cut me. I called you Jesus' son. In your unholy state, you carried it all. The way you busied yourself with dissecting the evil ones that walked in our path. You knocked down a few along the way. I want an in. All you offered was the absence of an entry point. The last chance I had of tasting heaven. I called you Jesus' son.

By Time, Sorrow And Life

I went home to visit my father and mother,
                                         their bodies
separated now—

I could not find my mother   behind the curtain

in the hamper with   the light shining

on its brown tones and wild flowers.
I could not find my father

sitting in the armchair with the cigarette lit,
reading the local sports section of the paper.

I went back home to visit the ones that gave birth
to them. Their bodies, long gone. Death

abides by laws of decomposition,
regretful tears. A salt bath,

I thought. If I could suspend
my body, my breasts
could defy gravity.

I Am My Father's Daughter

What was it about the silence? When the pig died, yells and squeals subsided. When planes did not fly so close above our heads. What was it that made it memorable? You put toothpaste on my toothbrush and mint went into my eye. I smiled through the pain. I wanted to cry. Was it always this way? My stomach cannot dunk its roundness underwater. This is how I rebel against gravity these days, through my plumpness. Roundenss. Unapologetically I expand to what I only used to dream of: being
                    a complete woman.

I visited the grave of my grandparents. No! In fact I have never sat on the bench by their gravesites. I just wanted to take in the smell of the two homes one more time. The fried bread smell down the hall from the kitchen always traveled into the front of the house. Quiet on my walk through the walls of time that hold our secrets. Their secrets are hot tea cups with vapor rising, the sting of burning tongues speed to taste sweetness. I wanted to taste their pain. Their loss and travails. I know then I loved. Loved from my center and encompassed all of them. The orphans in my family. Grandma Ilush was a puzzle never to be solved. Grandpa Dedi, would carve a home inside my soul and burn in my memory.

I remember him for the first time: tall, bald, unadorned, smelling of sweet sweat, raging alcoholic breath. His fist would pound on our kitchen table long after he decomposed inside the Romanian earth where he is buried. I long to hear his voice again, even yelling. To see his almond eyes with yellow hollows around the red rims. The blue never shied away from pain, like water they reflected it to little old me.

As I walk through our home of 13 years, I want to remember the yells that went unanswered, tears that went unseen, pain that went unfelt. Unsheltered, unfiltered, in the (un)making/undressing.

Generations now course through the veins of Olivia and Luna. Buni Ilush's ghost face in the baby Olivia, for the first few years. Dad calls her my daughter. I have my grandmother's body, the curves, the starting-to-droop breasts with large areolas. Hips that could carry a baby. The pan in my hand, in our basement apartment with only slivers of light drawn on the floor.

What was I doing there in the deadly silence of the day? Reconstructing all of us as I felt death stealing you away. I tried to rebuild the shape of love. I tried to remember the smell of your skin in summer after the sun hit it for hours. Pores ready to receive, sweat beads on the surface. My forehead and upper lip still sweat like my Uncle Ica's.

I disappointed him with my double chin. My belly could be misconstrued as being 6 months along a line I've never been on. *Do you love me, daddy?* I come to visit you as I am. The body of my grandparents.

I am my father's daughter.

My Fear, My Butcher, My Love

The thought of you sends shivers through me. Monumental, as you were—to stop you was insane. You fed hundreds. Your work: our existence. It is no coincidence. We were trapped. Since when is communism not oligarchy? It feels the same. Insane, how long this went undetected. The necks you claimed—too many to name. And names—what am I saying? The animals had none. The pigs, my friends, I knew by their snouts, their squeals, the blotches on their skin. I never imagined stepping into their skin while chewing on an ear, a tail, after the curtain fell. I am not desperate for you to listen. I count the days since those days—not glory, just sinners thriving in the past. 13,514 days separate me from the first time I feared you. Loved you. Was fed by you.

There was a closet of knives. Sharpened weekly. Wielded like swords with reverence. Blades thin as whispers. Shrieks sharp as memory. The passion. The punishment. The way I like to be slapped on my derriere. A cocktail, filthy and cold—like a dirty martini shaken with bone dust and brine. Punishment, served with a twist. My back breaks—twice—along this path. In the high courts they will ask: "Was your back already broken?" To which I'll respond: "You try carrying carcasses—hundreds—their deafening squeals enough to drown a city like Bucharest, where the concrete still remembers."

And their names—yes, each one had a soul. Named for angels. Prophets. Martyrs. Their beautiful names I will recite before the judge. For that, I thank my butcher. My love. My terror. He put me in hell only to sustain me until I met you—my love.

I Pray For Sinners

I pray for the sinew of sinners, since no one else would. He was the furthest from it—a saint in his neighborhood, of his own making? He was not delusional; his strength outlasted most. In the coma that lasted weeks, on the bed he died and sinned in, the lifereel played and replayed. Nobody could save him. Not even himself. I did not know he was dying. I was in college when I was told he had been comatose. I pray for his hands in the afterlife—not to have to break through so many table tops, so many walls, scratching his knuckles to the bone. I pray he is as seen, with a sea of eyes upon his flesh, as he offers gifts of gold and rose petals to the onlookers. I pray he is as understood as he is understated, while placing upon the butcher's block the books his granddaughter has written. Ahead of his time, he was a peacemaker, a pleaser, a feeder. His lean physique should not have been mistakenly taken for granted; he was a force to be reckoned with. Strong warrior against the hunger of an entire nation under communism. They stole our food, our electricity, our heat and water, our dignity, our children—while he was a provider and a restorer of all that was lost. Nothing could stop him. I believed him as soon as he opened his mouth. I was a few months old when we inherited each other. Our lives were to overlap for thirteen years thereafter. That is it. As I sit here at the age of fifty, and Dedi is long gone, I reflect upon the ricochet of this early life experience. Yet the reverberations are of such intensity that the experience erases itself from memory—to save its own ass. I was asked by the professor at the Bowery Poetry Club, "So do you write about Romania in your books?" It is the only thing I write about, I told him. The land of all my beginnings, the inherited endless lines that never merge into highways but stay off the beaten path. This is my past that informs my present. I am forgetting how to address my elders in Romanian, for I am now that older and wiser audience member.

Acknowledgments

This book would not exist without the enduring love and support of my family—especially my mother, Georgette, for her strength and artistry, and my father, who carried us across continents to a new life.

To Michael, my love and anchor, thank you for believing in me through every draft, every silence, and every breakthrough.

Deep thanks to Alisha for her brilliant vision for the cover and for championing this book to the finish line with grace and care.

To my teachers, friends, and readers who walked with me on this journey—your voices echo in these pages.

And to the ghosts—thank you for letting me tell our story.

To Heather Baillie Young

Your brilliance, patience, and tireless encouragement have been the foundation upon which this book stands. With your insight and gentle guidance, you brought clarity to my tangled words and breathed life into my vision. The Butcher's Granddaughter is as much yours as it is mine—a testament to your faith in this story and your unwavering belief in me. For every edit, every suggestion, and every moment you dedicated to shaping this work, I am profoundly grateful. Thank you for being the true partner this book needed.

To Alisha Hawrylyszyn Frank

Thank you for your extraordinary eye and intuitive brilliance. Your vision for the cover brought this book to life in a way that felt both haunting and true. You understood the spirit of the work from the very beginning and translated it into an image that holds the story's weight and mystery. But your contribution didn't stop at design. You championed this book from start to finish with quiet strength, steady belief, and a deep respect for what it was trying to say. Your guidance was not only editorial and aesthetic, but emotional—reminding me again and again that the story mattered.

I am deeply grateful for your clarity, your care, and the heart you brought to every step of this journey.

Adela Sinclair is a NYFA (New York Foundation for the Arts) Grant winning Romanian-American poet, translator, and teacher. Fluent in English, French, and Romanian, poetry is her primary, though not exclusive, medium. Her chapbook entitled *LA REVEDERE* is now available through Finishing Line Press. Her poetry explores themes of cultural identity, memory, loss, trauma, and desire. Her work appears on *"The Bridge,"* published by Brooklyn Poets, and Tupelo Press' *"30/30 Project."* "On April 26, 1986, Chernobyl Exploded", Adela's poem is published in the Winter Anthology *Healing Felines and Femmes* by Other Worldly Women Press. She has performed her poetry all over New York City including the Yale Club, 92nd Street Y, Bowery Poetry Club, Poet's House, Brooklyn Poets, Books are Magic, KGB Bar, Saint Francis College, and Writer's Voice at the JCC. She is a founding member and poetry editor of the emerging literary magazine, *Unbound Brooklyn*, and volunteers with Ugly Duckling Press in Brooklyn. Adela holds a BA in French Culture and Civilization from SUNY Albany, with additional coursework at the Sorbonne University of Paris, an MA in Education from Hunter College (NYC), and an MFA in Creative Writing/Poetry from St. Francis College (Brooklyn).

www.ingramcontent.com/pod-product-compliance
Lightning Source LLC
Chambersburg PA
CBHW030058170426
43197CB00010B/1580